Groanings from the Desert

A collection of English & Spanish teo-poemas,
prayers, & thoughts

By
Alma Lizzette Cárdenas- Rodríguez

Kissi,

thank you
for your continued
support through the
different phases of
my crazy life.
Hope you are living
your best life &
dreams. ♥

Alma
Lizzette (R).

Preface

Long trenzas and outfits made by my mom's or tia's hands is how I remember my sister and I. There is another childhood detail I will never forget, I would tell others that I wanted to be a lawyer when I grew up. I have always had a passion for pursuing what's right. My teenage years choice of music affirms this further. I listened to "rock en español" what my mother and church tradition called demonic. For me, the lyrics were more in alignment with Jesus and love than the church community and its people ever were. The lyrics spoke of injustice and the ills of society, while church was more about throwing pain and reality under a rug.

Growing up under the pews of a Latino protestant community was filled with joy and mourning. Joy because it was where I experienced community and laughter, where I witnessed miracles as I saw all helping hands come together to help just one. But painful because it was a culture which constantly reminded me what was wrong with me instead of affirming my talents and gifts. Their thinking that reflected unity as uniformity never felt or fit right.

The same spirit of justice and righteousness was probably in my maternal abuela Lencha as well. I will never forget the day I talked to my mom about the movie "COCO". I asked her why she never taught us the beauty of our culture which this movie revealed. She shared that Dia de los Muertos and some of the other traditions were taught in the context of the Catholic Christian religion that her mom had never inculcated in her. The reason was that my grandma had been fed up with the Catholic Priest always trying to forcibly kiss her. So as a resistance, she stayed away from all things church building and its traditions. Here I am thirty six years later, staying away from all things church buildings and toxic traditions. I had more in common with my grandma than I ever knew. Now I mourn that I could never turn back time to hear the stories of my grandma from her account; wondering if she would have ever been willing to share such stories with me. That was the moment I realized, this story cannot repeat itself. I want to share with my children parts of me, the disappointments, the victories, all of it. I want Esther and Abigail, my daughters, to have this first account. So that one day as they tell their own stories, they'll be able to talk about their crazy outspoken mother's heart. In the process I felt led to open this collection as a door to my home, and welcome you to my living room as you read through the pages of this book.

"Groanings from the Desert" is a sacred place that holds pieces of me that are scary to share, but deadlier to think that I am alone and keep them to myself. This collection of teo-poemas, prayers, and thoughts invites you into my pain, joy, hopes, and dreams. They were written between February and October of the year 2020. Writing them has released my voice in a way I never knew was in me. This in turn has allowed me to heal and step into being fully me. This book is especially for our youth, young adults, and women of color, but also for their parents, mentors, pastors, madrinas, and padrinos who are walking alongside them. May you always have people around you who create spaces that encourage you to speak, dream, and be unapologetically you.

Thank you for the opportunity to stand at the door of your mind and hearts home.

With gratitude,

Alma Lizzette Cárdenas-Rodríguez
Sun Valley, CA

Acknowledgements

A village of support whose hard work and inspiration has led me here cannot go unnamed. First I want to thank my husband Sergio Rodriguez and our daughters Esther and Abigail. Sergio, thank you for always supporting my thoughts and work, even when we butted heads. For helping edit this book, for saying yes to journeying, learning, and unlearning with me. To all three of you for your patience and care for me over the last years, I love you.

To my mom Teresa Vargas, your prayers never went unheard. I believe I am still alive today because of them. To my siblings Ruth and Alberto Cardenas, and my dad Alberto Cardenas, thank you for all you are and for loving me at my best but also at my worst, which I know was painful to you all (especially our mom).

To my best friend Mayra Rios, for your unwavering friendship and for being a safe space since I was 21. Your family and you have always been a tangible reflection of God's heart in my life.

To my Fuller Youth Institute (2015), and Azusa Pacific University MATUL (2018) professors, cohorts, and program managers, I am here because you all contributed to my growth and set the spaces for thinking, and the releasing of my voice.

This last year I am thankful to the Puente, Alegria Publishing, and Fuller Formation communities and retreats where I have found sacred space and God outside of what I had known. Davina Ferreira your mentorship leaves large shoes to fill, for those of us who intend to mentor with our heart, to follow.

To the women of Sweet & Profane, and the mujeres in Pasadena, California whom I've had the pleasure to work with and learn from. Our dreams and work has not, and will not be in vain.

To the Sun Valley youth and young adults, of the formerly known as Aposento Alto church, that Sergio and I helped organize and lead for many years. Thank you for your prophetic voice, dreams, and gifts. You were the inspiration behind many decisions I have made and the values I hold dear today. It was bittersweet to witness with my own eyes as I saw you evolve, grow, and learn from you, that something different is possible.

To God, I know you had everything to do with this village of support and with connecting all of us together, each in due and perfect season, for such a time as this. ¡Gracias!

ISBN:978-1-7347252-7-8
Book Design: Sirenas Creative
Cover Art: Ruth Cárdenas | @culturalvibrasla
Publisher: Alegria Publishing
Printed in the United States of America

"Y no se adapten a este mundo, sino transfórmense mediante la renovación de su mente, para que verifiquen cuál es la voluntad de Dios: Lo que es bueno y aceptable y perfecto."

Romanos 12:2 (NBLA)

"There is no greater agony than bearing an untold story inside you"

Maya Angelou

I'm unfolding my thoughts

I folded my thoughts
like a note on a paper
to store them in the back of my mind
where no one would ever read them,
and now I'm questioning, why?

36 years old,
and realizing there are too many spiderwebs,
in the library of my folded notes.
I have decided to dust them off, crack them open,
and gift what's still left of them to the world.

¡Mujer!

¡Mujer! I am not more or less than anyone else.

I am brilliant.
I should be listened to for what I have to say,
and not by how I look or what I wear.

I am a mother and wife.
They are gifts and not labels
that give any status quo permission
to confine me to a box, to an end all be all,
or define God's purpose for my life.

Made in the image of God.
One of the characteristics describes God as a lion,
el Leon de Juda.
In the animal kingdom lions will not survive
without the lioness. She is the hunter.
Taking initiative for the nourishing
of her family is in her blood.
If women are made in the image of God,
then initiative for the nourishing of her family
is too in their blood.
What mujeres have to contribute is nourishing
for the present and the porvenir
of our families and comunidad.

We were conditioned to believe that
happily ever after was when the princess found her prince.
But happily ever after
is something else, so much more.
It is in exercising our God given gift
of taking initiative,
and our God given gift of choice.
It is in the unlocking of our unique voice
and encouraging joy in the midst of the noise;
for the collective well-being of us as a whole.

I stand on the shoulders and wisdom of mujeres like my mom,
las hermanas de la Iglesia, the women of our families,
some no longer living on earth with us.
They have modeled strength, resilience, faith,
truth, and justice with hands and heart.

I have two young girls and I am so tired of hearing,
you should shoot for the boy!
Who will carry on the last name?
It will make you whole!
But I am complete.
I don't care about carrying the legacy of a last name
from generation to generation
or fitting the mold of a perfect family
in a culture's expectation.

Mujer, may knowing you are made in the image of God,
where you are going, as you unpack where you have come from,
be like a rooster crow whose sound awakens in the morning,
and cause in you a new awakening every time.

living through change

There is nothing more uncomfortable
than living through change.
Welcoming new rhythms.
Accepting a different normal
because some things will just never be the same.
Molding yourself into a new seat
in a completely new space.
Knowing that anything can change at any moment once again.

Boundaries

To say yes to you
You may have to say no
to the expectations of others.
Go, be brave
Set your boundaries in place.

Profeta

Hay profetas de nombre, que se pasean en avión.
Que vuelan sobre pueblos, pero desconocen su valor, su dolor,
y el llanto de su corazón.

Si alguna vez lloraron, se les olvidó.
Y si alguna vez dolieron, el llegar tan alto los entumeció.

También hay profetas no de nombre, pero sí de corazón.
No reconocidas por humanos, pero ungidas de Dios.

Cuando hablan a los "grandiosos" se asombran en temor.
Porque su voz suena al tono de justicia, verdad, y valor.

Amanece con el llanto del pueblo.
Descansa al saber que sola no está.
Por que con el pueblo vive el dolor.
Y cada mañana se alimenta
en saber que el pueblo aunque humilde es importante.
Y en su corazón siempre está.

Cuando la mires por la calle preguntale como está,
porque a veces se esconde y vive en soledad.

Desfallece al oír que nada nunca cambiará,
pero le trae fuerzas saber que la miras y que sola no está.

13

Tiempos de incertidumbre

Tiempos de incertidumbre, llegaron como un temblor.
Nadie se lo esperaba, y sin planearlo llegó,
Con su movimiento llegó inseguridad.
Queriendo robar el aire, queriendo aplastar la paz.

Pero cuando me siento y respiro,
el miedo de las noticias como una nube se va.
La ansiedad en mi cuerpo empieza a desvanecer,
y una vez mas deja descansar.

Esto me ayuda a enfocarme en otra realidad.
A darle freno a el pecado de siempre querer hacer
cada vez más y más.
Me lleva a poner la vista en lo que en la vida importa más.
La familia, salud, y vivir el momento que no promete siempre estar.

Salir afuera a disfrutar el aire,
y cada dia dar gracias a la nueva oportunidad.

Dar bienvenida a tener tiempo para salir a caminar.
Y con Dios encontrarme, Su voz escuchar.
Ver a los pájaros volando sin preocupar.
Y vivir en la esperanza que como a los pájaros Dios nos cuidará.

Que impulsa a recobrar valentía, y salir a volar.
A la dirección del aire y la visión de Dios
que con Su creación alguna vez te mostró.
Con una ala llamada fe, y la otra sueños.
Que la realidad de la tierra nunca te los venga a desplumar.
A volar con la esperanza de que algún día de la fe
y los sueños algo florecerá.

Prayer of mercy

God of mercy, God of all
Tú que reinas en el cielo y en la tierra
Tú que viniste para amar y sanar al enfermo

We ask for mercy
To you who has the power and spirit to move in ways not humanly possible

We cry:

Clear the airwaves of our bodies
Bring to light the obstruction, so that it can be treated
Bring to light our destructive ways
That it would be healed, made whole,
and move in its intended function

As many experience this through our bodies
by the pandemic of Covid 19
May the institutions and systems that have us gasping for air
experience the same

We cry:

Clear the airwaves of our governing bodies
Bring to light the obstruction, so that it can be treated
Bring to light our destructive ways
That it would be healed, made whole,
and move in its intended function

Líbranos de esta enfermedad
For the well-being of all, especially the most vulnerable among us

Ten misericordia
God our healer

Amen.

Corazonada

Tengo la corazonada
que como una ola del mar,
esto pronto pasará.
A veces la ola deja sin aire,
a veces la ola quiere ahogar.
Pero nunca me doy por vencida,
y sobre el agua trato de flotar
para el aire volver a tomar.
Y después con toda energía
hacia la orilla empiezo a nadar.

Tal vez haya tragado mucha agua,
y con el sabor salado del mar
por un momento quedaré.
Pero se que más pronto que tarde
por la orilla del mar
volveré a caminar y continuaré.

Cruel

Cruel es la mentalidad de querer avanzar al costo de los demás
Cruel es querer abordar más de lo necesario
Cruel es tener y no dar
Cruel es saber y solo acumular conocimiento
Cruel es ver y no hablar
Cruel es dejar que el temor gane y no avanzar
Cruel...

Gratitud

Alguna vez Job le dijo a Dios:
"De oídas había oído de ti, y ahora mis ojos te ven"

Y ahora entiendo porque Job dijo eso
Al reconocer que mi vida ha sido tejida por tus manos Dios,
Aun cuando mis planes no han salido como los pensé
Y en esos momentos varias veces te cuestioné
Crei que quizas algo no había escuchado bien,
En tantos momentos pensé que te habías alejado
Pero siempre sabias lo que hacías
Porque siempre supiste lo que vendría después

Lo tenias fielmente calculado
Para que nada nos faltara o preocupara después
Tejiste mi vida de acuerdo a los tiempos
Porque en cada uno habría algo que aprender
Y todo para hacer este vaso más fuerte y brillante,
lista para cada después
A tus pies cada vez me sorprendes y aprendo,
y ahí quiero siempre permanecer.

Pendejismo is a choice

Pendejismo is a choice
Denying every learning opportunity to know
Saying no to the possibility to grow

Pendejismo is a choice
Closing its ears to the prophetic voice of our women and youth
Especially when it speaks truth to power
And cries on behalf of the most vulnerable

Pendejismo is a choice
Closing our eyes to the reality of one another
Just because the reality is not one's own

Pendejismo is a choice
Where the flow of comfort is easier than changing to the flow
of revealed truth

Pendejismo is a choice that we have all made
Pendejismo is a choice that we will continue to make
May we choose to intentionally unlearn from this and not make
pendejismo a recurring mistake.

RIP to raising our hands to speak

When I was a child, Sunday and elementary school teachers
Told us to raise our hand and wait our turn for an opportunity to speak

Often overlooked, I blamed it on me
And slowly but surely, I stopped raising my hand for a chance to speak

Until one day a beautiful soul taught me it was a system so that my
voice could remain shut and closed

I was 32, crying from anger while others unaffected laughed in the back
That day I vowed to do differently and speak without raising my hand

While I would like to say I've been successful
That pattern has been hard to unlearn
And the same ugly system is now taught to our own children at schools

I can't change a system but I can change what I do at home
So for now I will remind my daughters that when they need to speak,
have a question, or need to express a thought,
they don't need to wait a turn or raise their hand

The goal is that one day it would be normal
to make space for all to speak.

Aromas del ayer

Quarantined and working from home
has been a life-giving gift as there
is time write thoughts,
and cook in between.

Los frijoles de la olla are now on low heat.
The arising smell makes me hungry,
currently taking me back in time to many memories.

Memories, like a day in Mexico
standing in my grandma's front yard
I must have been 6 or 7 years old
in a humble home on
the hills of San Miguel, Durango, Mexico.

As I played on the dirt
with the different kinds of animals roaming around,
my grandma showed up with an ax
to cut a chicken's head off
I stood there in awe
as the scene unfolded before my eyes,
watching the chicken run headless
for a few minutes before it collapsed.
I'll never forget,
I did not eat dinner that night.

Memories, to the day when my mom
finally trusted me in the kitchen
with her guiso on slow heat.
My only job was to turn off the stove
at the time she had instructed me.

When she came back home from running her errands
with my sister to their surprise,
they were greeted by black smoke
and the curtains seconds away
from igniting in fire.
Their screams woke me up from my nap,
and I was sad that I had let her down.

For a moment,
the aroma of the frijoles slowly cooking
took me to memories of the past.
It's an aroma that the busyness
and lack of life balance
had robbed me in years past
it had become easier to warm beans out of a can.

Quarantined and working from home
has been a life-giving gift.
Now I can't wait to eat my own cooked beans
for the first time in at least 3 years.

Lament

How much longer will you bind our backs with more work?
They feel like stacks of crates filled with rocks for little to no pay.

How much longer do these greedy systems think we can go, like a
headless chicken running around with no sight of a path or a road?
Speeding through, but chasing nothing for our dreams with the labor of
our feet and our hands.

How much longer will it be until our voices speak what our eyes see
and what our bodies feel?
How much longer will it be before these systems think of us and come
back to earth to walk with us, see what they have done, the harm, the
bloodshed, who like a river of tears rolls through our valleys?
Crying out of all the injustice

How much longer could we go pressed down this hard?
And be expected to continue to mow and grow to feed the mouths and
the pockets of the 1% at the expense of their own, with no end in sight.

How much longer?

It's never too late for justice

It's never too late for justice
It's never too late to do what's right
For as long as we are gifted with breathing,
the choice to right wrongs is alive

May our communities well-being propel you,
more than funders to keep your mission alive
Because then we will begin to flourish,
and reflect God's hands, feet, and heart

What good are the advocacy work claims,
when you strike your own staff and people
with the same oppressive rod that keeps our community in bondage,
with gates shut from abundant lands

You indulge in the brilliance of the vulnerable
You run with our thoughts as your own
To make matters worse you reward us nothing or much less
than you would an affluent guest

Next time you give us an offer
Would you stop to think,
would you say yes if the offer was for you?

Take these thoughts and know that we will love you,
but you must think of the collective good beyond you

It's never too late for justice
It's never too late to do what's right
For as long as we are gifted with breathing, the choice to right wrongs is alive.

Easter 2020

We are living somewhere between
the loss of life of Friday
and the uncertainty of Saturday...

Our faith's traditions would like us to be
on schedule with resurrection Sunday,
but we are not.

It will come,
but some of us are not there right now.

Wedding day

I am my own flower girl.
Yellow, red, pink, orange, and green petals
prepare the way of a path
which I have decided for me.

The path leads to an altar.
Where I will say yes to my dreams and gifts,
to learning and holding the imperfections of
the history of my community and culture
which weave me.

It is not picture perfect,
creation are my guests and witnesses.

For the first time in my life
I am owning my strengths, art, and beliefs.
Even when they are constantly shut down,
for being idealistic and too unreal to be.
The altar, a crossroads of my life.
Where I will commit not to one man or partner,
my vows are to me by me.

I promise to love you in success and in failures,
in sickness and in health. To receive every blessing just as you
have given. To be a voice of justice to the injustice we have endured
together. To embrace the different phases of yourself
in size 10,12,14, or 16. To strive towards what brings us equity of
wealth and health. To celebrate without regret every single victory,
and to mourn in times of loss without holding your volume down.
To be a voice of affirmation that blurs any sounds of condemnation.
And as you serve your family, friends, and comunidad, don't ever
again forget about you, that too is serving God.

Dressed in a rebozo, and equally proud in my skinny jeans
at 36 years old,
when some would say you are too old,
"ya se te pasó el tren"
this is my wedding day.
A commitment in perfect timing to me.
My rendition of a happily ever after, my American dream.

Maestra Abeja

Cuando el corazón humano se siente pesado
Y se encierra de su que hacer.
La naturaleza sale a tomar espacio
A trabajar lo que sabe hacer.

¿Alguna vez has puesto atención para ver?
A la abeja cuando sale a comer
y que con su polen a las flores y plantas ayuda a crecer.
Aún la semilla que trajo el viento
que en otro paisaje debía florecer
crece en tierra lejana, por el trabajo de la abeja
y brota sin que nada ni nadie la venga a entorpecer.

De su trabajo depende el fruto de la cual hemos de vivir y comer
Pero también la Maestra abeja nos deja mucho que aprender.

Que si como humanidad nos nutrimos mutuamente como la
abeja a las semillas, y ella de las plantas y flores.
Aun cuando el viento nos ha traído de diferentes paisajes.

Dicho de mi ama

Cuando éramos niñas, a veces nos daba flojera buscar algo perdido.
Y mi amá siempre nos decía,
"Si quieren encontrar las cosas, las deben salir a buscar
Las cosas a ustedes, no las van a venir a encontrar."

Sus palabras siempre hacían retumbar las paredes.
Y hasta este día a los tímpanos de mis oídos
sus enseñanzas vienen a tocar.
Me recuerdan del trabajo que requiere de mi parte tomar,
si mis metas quiero alcanzar.
Y que con mis palabras y mis manos puertas debo salir a tocar.

"Si quieren encontrar las cosas, las deben salir a buscar
Las cosas a ustedes, no las van a venir a encontrar."

Moral injury

Moral injury in me is like
a fruit plant confused by the water it was fed to keep it alive
Because it never knew it was mixed with herbicides
that have kept her from growing and nourishing in her fullest
flavors, smells, and shine

She has been told to give as she has been given
But how can she give something that instead of life
is actually killing?

Moral injury caused by religious institutions
who fed me lies for truth
Whose examples of loving had nothing
to do with the words that came out of their mouths

Is a confusing water that had numbed me from my best life.

Idea of a pulpit reconstructed

The pulpit to turn my ear to is not man made
It is not limited to a building, it doesn't sit on a church stage

The pulpit to pay attention to, is the dirt of mama Earth
She speaks through every seed
When I sit to watch them birth, live, and grow

From the tiniest to the largest, she welcomes us all
The pulpit to turn my ear to, sprouts from mama Earth's lands.

Devastating

Devastating is when our communities of faith
have been willing to engage in conversation
when I say the word fuck or when I say the word shit

But not willing to engage in conversation
at the profanity of human rights violations
And call dehumanizing leaders and systems
righteous and God sent.

lost poet

Born with an imagination and a flow of words that never ran out
My first grade teacher always told mom, she's great,
but she talks too much in class
The instructions before going to visit anyone were:
don't ask for anything, sit down, and stay quiet

After some time, like wine
her questions and words aged in a bottle
Until education revealed her freedom to think
Uncorking and releasing a smell of beauty and wild

A red blend of rage, cry, and hope
Aged groanings turned to words
Finally landing on a page written down
as poems, prayers, and thoughts
Yearning to be read and heard to those willing to try
Like I would a red blend glass of wine
In hopes that their smell and taste will resonate
with at least one other human soul

A lost Poet, whose words have been uncorked is now found
And she will write and share
until the day her vineyards words like grapes are no more.

De la tierra

Como el agave con mucho sol, y poca agua he crecido
Y mi madurez continúa siendo una larga jornada.

Pero aunque viva mis días bajo el sol, y con muy poca agua
Sé que algo lindo aunque filoso crecerá.

Gracias a Dios y a la creación
cuyo arduo trabajo han sido como el trabajo de un/a jimador/a.

Que al llegar su tiempo la piña completa
de este agave finalmente se descubrirá.

Y algo dulce e irreverente pero sanador de ella se exprimirá.
Y como el agave hijuelos de ella saldrán y crecerán.

Vulnerability

Vulnerability, you are a draining task. Like a farmer tending to a field, patiently recognizing and removing the good weeds from those that block. Separating the weeds from the blooms to make sure it is not deprived of what it needs to survive. To make sure it yields what it is meant to grow and rise.

Vulnerability, you are a laborious task. At the end of a day with you, all I want to do is sleep, sit in the dark silent, and hope for a morning to once again see the sun shine.

A cry of a Millennial Latinx who grew up under the pews of a church

We are here
We are talking
Is anyone hearing?
Is anyone watching?
Is anyone catching our words?
The hurt that we hold
The hurt that we feel
Like a cut across the throat

Are you paying attention?
The earth is speaking, are you willing to hear?
Youth like blooms are dying
Some are running out of strength but trying
New ones from faraway lands are sprouting

On this lays my hope
Our creative has a story to tell
A present and future reimagined
With all the energy to resist the urge
of another generation's stories going unheard,
or going unseen

Will you see us?
Will you hear us?
Will you include us?

We are doing it with or without your stamp of approval
But with all the approval from God.

A never forming scar

I am floating on a river of tears,
brought by wounds whose dry skin continues to be peeled.
To reveal blood as an ocean so large,
it has no beginning or end,
as I hardly reach to see from shore's sight.

A scar that never gets a chance to form.
The pain is like an expectation, a normal thing to feel.
Caused by the never ending wounds of injustice.

Sister

If sister were a verb it would be the act to heal.
As we stepped in each other's shoes
and were brave enough to walk in each other's heels.
It would mean to be part of each other's lives, and be so intertwined, that
we would walk past the labels, that the status quo constantly tries to define.

¿De cual agua vamos a tomar?

Esos ojos de color, que nuestra gente anhela tener
Como que fueran el más preciado regalo,
como si fueran mejor que los de color café.
¿Por qué?

A la blanquita la llamamos bonita
A la morenita, pobrecita.
¿Por qué?

A lo negro lo asociamos con malo
A lo blanco como el grado más alto a obtener.
¿Por qué?

¿Qué estamos diciendo?, ¿Que nos estamos enseñando?

Tenemos opciones,
ignorar o aprender,
conformismo o reformismo,
muerte o vida,
El bien de las mismas personas, o el bien para toda la humanidad.

Las vidas y el porvenir de mis hermanos y hermanas negras importan.
¿De cúal agua vamos a tomar?
¿De cúal agua vamos a dar?

El libre albedrío tenemos
Para escoger entre ser agentes de justicia o ser cómplices del mal.

Bold prayer

May God bring to light
the toxic we have learned that has led our mind
to think black lives are worth less than anything white
to believe that a burned building is more important than a human life
to repent and ask forgiveness for giving in to those lies.

May there be breakthrough in our minds
That mobilizes actions across the lines
To be willing to make friendships where there once was divide
So that our children will see a different world as we raise them
Amen.

I am drained

I feel like I have been swimming under the sun all day.
Thirsty, with my skin red in pain.

From swimming in the waters of having to explain.
To a pool filled with people whose ears are covered in plugs,
only pretending to hear, and not willing to engage.

I need a break, I am hungry, all I want to do is sleep.
And I wonder, when do I know it's time to pass the torch to whoever
is next to swim in this space to justice?

I am drained.

Solidarity

Solidarity
Easy to say, hard to do.

Like a dance, it takes two.
Two people, that may be different in thought,
culture, color, or music preference.

As one person follows, the other one leads,
and at times the leader will also have to teach.
The roles interchange,
leading and following is not attributed
to one or the other.
It is willing to give,
as much as it is willing to receive.
The partnership does not have to end when the song is over.

What if solidarity was a lifelong dance?
Which in turn gave life to another tune, or a new dance move.

What if the only way to add to my life was to subtract from it?

If the only way to add to my life was to subtract from it,
I would unwind from the idea that life is made
from grand moments witnessed by large crowds.

I would remember that my most precious moments
are in the day to day routine of life.
In the interactions where I can share the best of me,
and encourage thinking and love.

I would subtract the people who continually drain,
by perpetuating a culture that needs to be about fame.

Childlike

I want to emulate my daughters fearlessness,
For their ability to jump off places,
without a consequence in mind.

Replicate their voice that cries,
when something is not right.

Like a child, without a worry,
always curious to learn and open to trust.

Like a child, play, and create with no end in sight.
Without being distracted by keeping track of time.

Fear locked

You are good enough,
Repeated my inner voice

And fear had no choice but to close its mouth,
to hide behind closed doors

Affirmations are like a key that locks away all fear.

Welcome home

Welcome home.
Where thoughts are unrestrained
A voice is never tamed
Breasts unlock from the torture of bra
Where feet are untied to set themselves,
as they were meant, on the ground.
From where all living things come,
and find balance between work and rest.

Strong

Inspired by a Julia Alvarez quote:
"El papel lo aguanta todo"

I used to think the strongest could carry heavy weight.
I used to think the strongest were made of protein and muscle.

Now, I realize the strongest item I know weighs little in
comparison to the things expected to carry the most.
Paper, you are the lightest,
but yet carry the weight of the ink that paints the heaviest
thoughts, cries, experiences, questions and fears.

Strong you've been redefined, by a sheet of paper.

Tending our mind like our ancestors tended fields

What if we tended to our mind,
as our ancestors tended to fields?

And we were open to fires,
the kind that burns everything to the ground
Which prepares the soil for new seeds.

Seeds of truth.
Watered by our collective repentance, and lamentation.
Which as a result brings forth new fruit.

Fruit without GMO,
with out modified histories
that minimize stories of our own.
Which have been like pesticides,
systems that continually ill
to eventually kill.

What if we tended to our mind,
as our ancestors tended to fields?

Malcriada

Malcriada was a word I heard from my mom
usually followed by a nalgada.
Malcriada was a word used to describe me
when I broke the rules.
When I responded to an unfair reprimand,
also known as talking back.
When I just wanted to say hi from afar
and not come into a room to shake everyone's hand.

I now realize that I was not being a malcriada.
I was exercising my God given gift to make decisions of my own
I was not being a malcriada,
I was simply refusing to go with the flow
It was a glimpse of my future
It was the seed of contracultura,
setting its roots under the ground that no one saw,
including me.

If you asked me now, where you being a malcriada?
I would say,
Malcriada,no.
Contracultura,si.

My biggest fear

Becoming the oppressive leader who silenced
and suppressed the gifts I had to bring is my biggest fear.

The only way I can think to disarm it,
Is to tell people of how that truly feels.

Remember those painful memories,
Acknowledge the space they held.
Name the feelings, and not be afraid to share.

The only way I can think to disarm it,
is to be leaders that will allow ourselves to be called out.
By our children, youth, and community,
the voices often left in the backs of lines.
Not allowing us to throw the mistakes or questions under a rug.

Keeping each other grounded,
when that ego tries to blow our head up and off the ground,
and avoid seeing how history is repeating itself with one's life.

Deep breath

As I take a deep breath in
& release breath out

I welcome you Spirit of God.
I make room for airways that were caused by tension
of weakness trying to usurp itself as might.

As I take a deep breath in
& release breath out

I am allowing my body to say the prayers
that my mind can't always wrap itself around
to bring to words what is held deep inside.

Al fin pare, y profundamente respire.
Aunque no es costumbre
el detenerse del que hacer.
Me di cuenta de la necesidad de tenerlo que aprender.

Sweat

Sweat is the cry of hard work.
Of a muscle growing as it is being challenged to labor,
outside the routine of its day to day chores.
Going past the limits of what it has known.
Consistently.
Sweat drops are waters that will reap growth.

Slow motion

In a rushed world, an act of resistance will be to slow down.
It feels wrong.
As if I am not doing enough.
But as I am growing, I understand that the best contribution
to my community during the never ending tumultuous times
Will
Be
To
Take
Care
Of
Oneself.
You are not slow motion.
It's just a rhythm of what is humanly possible.
Previously known as not enough.

©vid-19

What if this moment was calling us to a child's pose?
To position us to be willing to re-learn, not walk on our own.
But trust others to be held
To be fed and wiped down in our shittiest parts.
As something normal that a caregiver does with love.

What if this moment was calling us to a child's pose?
A student at the feet of a teacher,
To present ourselves as a blank slate.
To learn differently according to the times.

What if this moment was calling us to a child's pose?

Education

Pure, whole hearted teaching will want to see a student think
not force ideas into a mind.
An outcome could never be predesigned
because the journey will be left for the student to paint and define.

Papá

Papá, you are still and quiet like waters at bay.
Waters that were probably once in an ocean of storms,
of crashing waves.

I always wonder what your waters would say,
if you were able to speak of the storms
and the crashing waves you encountered out in the ocean
before they landed at bay.

Alma libre

Cuando una manera de pensar te mantiene aislada de lo que amas
y de la sociedad, eso se llama jaula con un letrero que para mi decía
iglesia haciéndose pasar por un sano hogar.
Al descubrir que sus reglas y pensamientos me enjaularon, y su
verdad nunca me llevó a la libertad.
Y la única llave que me ha ayudado para salir de esta horrible
realidad, para darle fin a las vueltas que me mantuvieron ocupada
sin avanzar, se llama voluntad.

Voluntad para preguntar,
y no tragarme todo lo que me daban de comer.
Voluntad para leer y aprender,
y entender más allá de lo que había conocido.
Voluntad para tomar el paso a salir,
y dejar espacios que nunca creerán en mí.
Voluntad para cortar con personas cuyos valores
no concuerdan con los míos.
Voluntad para decir adiós,
y darle la bienvenida a algo diferente.

Voluntad es la llave que hizo este alma libre para volar.

I am a writer

I am a writer
A plant who grew leaves, turned paper
Whose bloom's pollen turned ink
Sprouting from beauty others oversee and call dirt.

I am a writer
Refusing to white out, backspace, or press delete
To all the words that make up me.

I am a writer
I have written the notes at every meeting
Listening and writing from everyone else's thoughts and voices
Except from my own.

Waiting for a turn...
that was NEVER meant to come in boardrooms and meeting spaces.
But unknowingly preparing me to write the notes of my own
questions, thoughts, prayers, and voice.

My art

Complete yet growing
Multifaceted but unique
Like a naked body, revealing the curves,
the dips, and the flaws I call,
the beautiful pieces of me.
It does not fit into everyone's gustos or taste
Like meat is not digestible by a vegan or vegetarian,
I don't expect my art to be received by all.

But for me and maybe one other
It is a retreat from the noise inside.
And a retreat from the noise outside.

Not falling prey

When my intelligence is questioned once again,
and I am placed on a track expected to run, to win every race
In frustration I could do the predictable thing,
and throw words into the air, that are no different than the roar of a hungry prey
who waits for a dark time or my deep sleep to be bold enough to catch me
unaware as I lay in deep rest.

We can go in circles running life this way.
Or we can let the light that comes with every morning,
lead us to realize that we are not animals, to hunt or fall prey.
What we are is humans, and each other's kin.
If we truly knew this, instead of competing,
we could help each other succeed.
I am not falling prey to this game.

Footprints

If our footprints on the shore of a beach
can easily be washed away by a wave.
I wonder if lasting footprints, a legacy,
cannot be narrowed down to something visible.
What if footprints are more like an unforgettable experience
to be remembered in our hearts for the way it made us feel.

I am not a centerpiece

I am not a colored flower to fit a theme as
a party centerpiece.

Or a colored picture for a brochure of a mission that behind the
scenes is not what it seems.

Or a data number to mark the box that inclusiveness, diversity,
and equity is the reality of who you say you are
but yet are so far away.

I am not a centerpiece.

Losing labels

I am not generation trauma.
I am of a generation who is unwilling to hide
my truth and feelings under a rug.

I am of a generation who asks questions.
Questions that are not just making my head their home,
that would be taken to a grave untold.

I am of a generation who refuses to play actress
and say yes to a script that is far from relating to me.
The name of the play is assimilation.
That storyline is a maze which leads to a dead end,
to a destination titled "never reaching or exceeding expectations."

I am of a generation that will not bow down,
to make people or a system function in comfort,
at the expense of living as an imitation of someone who is not me.
I am losing the labels.

Educación

Educación es más que una lección
es un espacio
una habitación.

Se visita día tras día.
Incluso en días que traen con ella agonía.

Más que una lección,
la educación
es nutrición,
es mi pan de cada día.

Es una porción necesaria,
como la de los vegetales en mi plato.
Que mueve de mi cuerpo el desecho
y me libra de la enfermedad.

La educación es más que una lección
Es mi vitamina.

Detox

The thing about making the bold move out of toxic spaces is that,
while we lose friendships, and networks along the way,
and burn through bridges as people say.

Looking back it turns out they were just always in the way,
Not to help, but to keep my wings paralyzed and lead me astray.

And now we find ourselves making our own pathway.
Breaking out our own wings to move and fly on our own,
but together once again.

Repent and be saved

Repent and be saved were words
I heard repeatedly growing up.
Tract in hand, I saw my protestant Latina church family
say this to people in our community,
We were encouraged to repeat them to friends and family,
especially those who were not part of the
"goes to church on Sunday's band".

Everyone, including me, was a lost soul
in need of repentance and saving,
but now I wonder if we were the ones
misrepresenting God and misbehaving.

This thought, however, brings me to another point,
What if the only soul that needs to repent and be saved
is my own home?
The country that saw me grow,
the soul of the United States.
What if the souls in need of repentance and saving
are its people, countries, and faith communities
that adopted your ways?
As if it were something normal,
and something sane.

Who've drank your pills like vitamins
to result in strong bones.
But all you are is an eye sore,
a rotting collection of dry bones,
and hoarded horror stories not completely told.

United States, the country I have called home,
I wonder if you are the soul that needs to repent and be saved.
To one day truly be a land of the free,
and home of the healthy and sane.

Mentira

¿Que se le llama al orden que más bien trae desorden?
Mentira...

Mirrors/ Espejos

I have looked in a mirror every day,
Repeating patterns and routines,
seeing the same body and face.

But sisters, when I hear our stories,
they are like a mirror coming out of a closet,
Revealing parts of me that will never look the same again
showing me my different attributes and flaws along the way.
I see all of it,
the scars of painful moments that I had hid away.

My sister's mirrors are allowing me to see and feel once again.
Things I had never said out loud to my own face.
Their stories have been pivotal for me to heal in different ways.
May the story telling never end.
May our mirrors stand past the limits of time.
To reveal the beauty to our sisters for generations to come.

Amiga hermana.
Tu historia como un espejo que sale de un closet dentro de mi provoca
Descubrir partes de mi que no había visto con mis propios ojos,
O hablado de mi propia boca.
Que el contar nuestras historias nunca se acabe.
Y que a través de los tiempos nuestros espejos trascendan de
generacion a generacion.

Echate Porras

Have you been so busy
cheering for others,
encouraging others,
affirming the gifts in others,
that you forget to do that for you?

This is your reminder.
You are part of the whole.
And there's no we, without you.
Without your gifts,
we are like a puzzle incomplete,
missing a piece.

This is your reminder.
Échate porras.
Declara lo hermoso que hay en ti,
y confía en las destrezas que Dios ha puesto en ti.

let it shake

Have you ever noticed how your body shakes
when it is being challenged to stay in a form,
beyond what your body has known?

Have you ever noticed it's the same shake your body feels,
when you are about to partake
on an opportunity to speak,
as you stand on a stage or room filled with people
waiting to hear what you will say?

I am learning to let it shake.
Be okay with the gut twirls and aches.

Because this challenge
whether it's shaking your body or mind
is only a sign,
that you are stepping further into your design,
and that the shake is leaving weakness behind.
Building a muscle that will continually strengthen with time.

Let it shake.

2020 Vision

Soon we will breathe sighs of relief
even if the current situation is pure disbelief.

2020 is looking like it came to reveal
some blind spots
to give us a vision of what still needs to be
that is not yet.

It is positioning us to vote not for
one party or another
but to vote on behalf of the most vulnerable,
especially for our communities of color.

2020, you have brought to light the history
of the establishment of police.
To remind us that it needs to be reimagined
to something different
that may exist to build community trust and peace.

The world is watching.
Our youth are tired, speaking, and marching.
But more importantly our children are witness
to how we will be responding.

Police, my child admires you because she thinks you
take care of the world.

Let's not let them down,
2020 cannot just be another year that brought some things to
light
to then choose to live blinded, when 2020 is asking us to wake up,
and understand the times.

May we choose to be midwives to bring forth from 2020 new or
renewed vision.

Un recordatorio

La explicación la haré
en el nombre de traer mi perspectiva a una situación.

Pero nunca la haré
en el nombre del control.

Explicar a aquellos que vienen en nombre de control,
es como caer en la boca de un animal
Cuyo estómago no tiene fondo, no tiene final.
Su hambre, nunca se llega a saciar.
Y su mente no tiene la capacidad
de entender por la humanidad.

Explicar a aquellos que vienen en nombre de control
Exprime la energía.
Es perdida de tiempo
Nunca se llegará a un acuerdo
o a una sana solución.

Pero, explicar a aquellos que vienen en el nombre de perspectiva
puede traer alivio y alegría.

Da de comer tus palabras
a las bocas que están dispuestas a probar.
Y a estómagos que al final si se saciarán.

Memoria de Anthony McClain

Hermano,
la policía te mató sin razón.
Lo que te hicieron
no puede seguir recibiendo perdón.
No puede ser ignorado, o envuelto en algo normal
por el sistema que lo estableció y contribuyó.

Que tu muerte y la sangre derramada
de tus últimos momentos en vida
Que ahora pinta esta grama
Sea como lluvia que cae
en semillas de justicia.
Y que de ellas crezcan árboles que traigan
sombra y descanso a tu familia.

Que tu sangre derramada
traiga luz a la inmundicia.
La que ha crecido en el nombre de la avaricia.

Que su fruto nutra a tus descendientes
en el espíritu de justicia, amor, y verdad.
Y que ellos y ellas tengan la oportunidad de respirar
sin temer que alguien los o las vaya a matar.

Hermano, descansa en paz.
Mientras nosotros rompemos su disfraz
y desenmascaramos el antifaz.

Ants

When ants show up to my house
I freak out and hunt them down.

But now I wonder if it's just
God's voice through creation,
just wanting to have a talk
Inviting me to sit down.

To remind me that
a community works together to eat.

To remind me that
it takes all of our hands to make us complete.

To remind us that we may be small and unseen
but that we have a capacity to carry beyond
our own size for the comunal need.

To invite us to contribute our strengths and gifts
in community, if we are not already.
Even if it feels scary to be seen.

Si el cuerpo es un templo
#churchtoo

Si el cuerpo es un templo
en la Iglesia debe haber lamento
porque se han tratado los edificios
con más amor que las mujeres y niños
que pasan adentro.

Si el cuerpo es un templo
en la Iglesia debe haber lamento
que con él traiga un despertar
y avivamiento.

De que han tratado nuestros cuerpos,
como a un alimento,
algo que se come como a un pedazo de carne,
sin mente o conocimiento.

Las mujeres y los niños no somos objetos,
para placer visual o sexual.
Para saciar a depravados hambrientos.

Si el cuerpo es un templo
en la Iglesia debe haber lamento
que con él traiga un despertar
y avivamiento.

Depravación

Cuando una imagen
y pensamiento
entra a la mente
y baja al corazón
no hay capa ni falda tan larga
que pare una sucia acción.

When a woman speaks

When a woman speaks and asks questions
don't look at her like she is a fool
Listen to what she has to say,
and allow yourself to be schooled.

Church community reimagined

The church community spaces
I wish to help plant,
are not built on a brick foundation.
It is beyond the walls of a building,
with a huge fence installation,
and no human connection.

The church community spaces
I wish to help plant,
do not include people walking in
like robots on Sunday mornings.
Entangling in rhythms
that do not encourage collective,
or inner transformation.

The church community spaces
I wish to help plant and be a part of
take a whole other direction.
It starts with a small seed,
that requires our full attention.
It is committed to understand the past history
and present story of the soil under our feet.

It is not built with concrete blocks,
but by building relational interlocks.
Each of us is a bloom, or a component
which creates a beautiful landscape.

And the bloom does not feel more or less
than the soil in which it is grown.
It recognizes every one matters
to grow healthy and be.

The church community spaces I dream
are no longer a shallow store front.

leadership and titles

Leadership and titles are not
a free ticket into a person's life
It is not a key that opens a door
to an automatic trust

Leadership and titles are not
a magic wand that makes a person
unquestionable or untouchable

And although leaderships and titles may
come with a pay or ego raise
they do not make a person God.

Salvación

Salvación, ¿de qué me sirves para llegar al cielo?
Si la vida en esta tierra ya es un infierno.
De qué me sirve orar en el nombre de Jesús
Si las acciones de los que oran,
no son diferentes a los de Roma
y de Cesar en los tiempos de Jesús
¿Somos esclavos de la ley?
¿Agentes de justicia y sanidad?

Salvación, de qué me sirves para llegar al cielo
Si en la tierra no hay libertad
Cuando no hay la oportunidad para todos de
Ser dueño de su propio hogar
Si la tierra que se trabaja con tanto esfuerzo
es para darle a los mismos dueños comodidad.

Salvación, de qué me sirves si cuando estoy enfermo
para ir al doctor no tengo con qué pagar
Y que lo que gano y tengo,
en lugar de ahorrar a la iglesia taxes
vestidos de diezmo tengo que pagar
Mientras la Iglesia con sus bienes,
no siempre trae alivio a la comunidad.

Salvación de qué me sirves para llegar a un cielo
Si la oración que aprendí dice como en el cielo también en la tierra
Yo no espero la salvación en cielo,
sin haberla experimentado en la tierra primero.

Relief

When men police their minds and lives,
the way they police women, our bodies,
and our (fucking) time.

That will be a time when
women and children around the world
will experience relief.

Tragedy

A tragedy of our time,
is being comfortable with the instilling of fear.
Instead of bringing from out of the ground,
the dead roots that have made us dry.

Roots so dry,
we can't feel life bringing water even when it hits us.

Or much less to allow it to quench the thirst
or the waters to reach us.

Or embrace the heat of the sun like
hope brought by its light in between us.

That is a tragedy of our time.

What if eternal was not in heaven?

What if eternal was not a space?
What if eternal was a moment?

A moment where memories are created
Whose stories are passed down
from generation to generation

Making eternal not a place,
but memories, moments,
and stories for ever shared.

Cuando un tarro (frasco) se destapa

Cuando un tarro (frasco) se destapa
usualmente hay la confianza de que la etiqueta
de afuera indica lo que hay adentro.

Su envase usualmente descarga alimento
pero puede ser que más bien descargue un olor
que nos indica, que ya se pasó de su tiempo.

Pero a veces lo de adentro se deja salir
como una planta que estaba doblada
por mucho tiempo.
Porque habia crecido más alta y amplia
del espacio que le dieron por dentro.

Como una mujer que ha vivido encorvada
tener la oportunidad de estirarse.
Ver y caminar como siempre lo tuvo que
haber hecho, de pie.
Como algo nunca visto, un milagro.

Si la vida, la voz, y los sueños.
se dejarán destapar de un tarro.
Que revelaría lo que está por dentro?
Cuál sería su milagro?

O qué tal si miráramos a un tarro,
más allá de la etiqueta.
¿Cuál sería su hermoso regalo y legado?

Teamwork

What if team work was like a burpee
that requires the entire body to move.
Not all of it moves together at the same time,
but the body parts are guided to know
when it's their turn to move.

At times the feet will stay grounded
At times they will have to take a leap back
to then come back to front and ground.
Then there's a time where the upper body
takes the turn to help the body hold up.

What if team work was like a burpee?
We don't all move at the same time,
but we are aware when our turn to move is coming
and we all work together to move.

The result is always a stronger body
when it chooses to be consistent in its moves.

Forgiveness

Forgiveness is a journey, not a transaction
It's more complex than "forgive and forget"
Forgiveness is a journey where more than two are willing to--
bear with, feel with, see, and sit from the other person's seat.
It is not like forgiving a money debt.

Forgiveness is a journey, not a one day event
I now realize not everyone will choose to walk in this way.
But I rid myself of carrying all the weight
including the burden that belongs to people
who chose to not own up to their mistake, or walk away.
I have chosen to process and learn a lesson,
if there is anything left to take.

Because when a lesson remains,
it can be like used coffee grounds
which can fertilize a plant.
It's story can help another relationship
to be nourished, healthy, and grow.

Fallen leaf

If I was a fallen leaf from a tree,
I would like to be noticed by a child.

That the child would pick up and admire.
And ask all the questions of wonder,
like where the leaf's story began.

The child could hold the key to choose how this fallen leaf
continues, or if and when it ends.

Child, what will you make of a fallen leaf like me?

Was he really a betrayer?

We label Judas of the bible a betrayer
for selling his mentor Jesus to the system
that was threatened by his words and life

But now I wonder, if Judas was only doing what he was taught?
What he thought was right
following orders and following the laws

He walked with Jesus in a new kingdom way
But in the moment when it would have mattered the most
When the opportunity to make a different decision
than the one he had learned and been told
he missed it
He was not able to respond in the new kingdom way,
Even when he walked with him,
or if something had slapped him in the face
Wondering if recognizing that too late
was what led him to take his own life away

I hope we are able to recognize the Judas in our time
Doing what we thought was right
Following orders and following the laws

Praying that we don't recognize it when it's too late,
and that our response is to live differently and not take our own life away.

Pathfinders

I believe in a God--a creator who is a way maker.
But I also believe that we as creation are pathfinders.
We hold the key to find God's ways.
Without pathfinders, God's way making
is but a treasure waiting to be unlocked.
Without pathfinders willing to own their role,
creation is like a key sitting idle,
growing mold or tarnished, awaiting its purpose to unlock.

Poems

Poems are like music.
Each one carries a style, a tune
Sometimes an invitation to think or maybe to move.

Are all fires meant to be put out?

There are some flames that can't be blown out like a candle on a
birthday cake
They must be allowed to burn to the bottom, to take all the crop and
buildings in its way
To set the field for new foundations, and new seed that will only grow
with rest
Even if it means watching what you have worked so hard to build, burn to the ground.

I don't fear death

I don't fear death as much as I fear
not opening the door to a knock by the
opportunity to be made aware
and live the rest of my days
behind closed doors
in the comfortable warmth of my home

I hope my soul is able to recognize you
Like a camera on a front door
Every time you come knocking on this door.

Faces in horror

Like a ghost paled to white, colorless with sunken eyes
Present in place, but far away in mind
is the face not of a character from a horror movie or story

But a human face of another young black and brown child
who unjustly lost a father at the hands of a police officer.

Fall season

Some leaves are now falling from trees
that will never be the same

A tree releasing leaves
experiencing relief from weight
To rest, and take a break

To feel the wind
like a naked body, bare
without shame

Knowing that leaves and warmth
will come in due time once again.

Mis amigas

Estos días tengo a mis lados a dos fieles amigas
de un lado a Esperanza, y del otro a Lamento.
Cada una llama mi atención y pelea por mi tiempo.

Y aunque trato de balancear mi tiempo entre las dos
Últimamente mi tiempo se lo gana Lamento
que sin querer me suelta en llanto y agonía.

Por las mentes y la humanidad que no reconoce los tiempos
porque cada vez que siento la luz cerca,
la injusticia la viene a tapar.

Las dos son como un viento
Esperanza es como el relajante aire de un atardecer
y Lamento es turbulenta,
como el aire de una tormenta que no esperabas sentir o ver.

Las dos son diferentes
pero me recuerdan que sola no estoy
Y de dejarme sentir lo que se está viviendo.

A daily practice

For all the years I was encouraged to be strong
and move away from all my feelings

I will now allow myself to unleash every feeling
and every tear in the name of strength
as something normal and real

For as long as I need.

Cucarachas

Cucarachas can be killed one by one
especially when they come out at night.
You can do all you can to keep a house clean
to repel the cucarachas from coming back or in.

But I have learned that if you do not clean deep enough
to find the hidden nests
you can buy all the bug spray
and spend hours cleaning for them to stay away.
But the truth is that they will keep coming back
until you go deep enough to deal with the nest.

Cucarachas are like the pain life brings.
There is more to be explored underneath,
That we don't always immediately see.

Dry Bones

Growing up the prophet Ezequiel's passage
describing the valley of dry bones,
was used to teach us
to be quick to call the dry bones to life.
Without the invitation to wonder,
bring from under the rug,
or sit with the stories that left the bones to dry.
To be present like the prophet Ezequiel,
before skipping to bringing them to life.

I am not the prophet Ezequiel.
But I too sit surrounded by valleys of dry bones of
racism, social inequity, homophobia and gender inequality.
And I wonder if before we are quick to call solutions to life
we need to accept the invitation to show up
and sit with the stench, and the stories
which brought them in the first place to dry.

That's the only way dry bones with long term dignifying solutions
will ever come to life.

Kids Menu

The kids menu at a restaurant is like toxic education
Teaching my child to circle the butterfly
that was different from a group pictured
Instead of teaching my child to recognize how they are alike,
how they are unique.
And then we wonder why we treat each other the way we do as human beings.

Patterns

I have learned that patterns will paralyze,
and keep you on your knees for as long as you
don't decide to think, and do something different

In submission to people and ideas too threatened
to see you step into your purpose in life
keeping you on the edge of a cliff
to keep you too afraid to move on

I have learned that the toxic patterns
will keep one living on different extremes
without worry about how it affects the people
who lie in between

Extremes that teach you that serving others before yourself
is the right way, at the expense of your body spirit and mind
Until you awake like a bug in a spiderweb with little time
to unwind before you are eaten

Until you catch the lie
And realize you were a butterfly in a cocoon at the edge
Growing her wings that would push her
To be free to fly
For when the time came to get off her knees,
she would no fall off the cliff
she would not die

She would just break a pattern
when she had faith strong enough to know
that God also created a season where she would have
to decide for herself to break her wings out

To 8 year old Alma we are safe
We are living a truth, and broke a pattern
which fills our soul and set us to fly free.

Write your vision

This book is a manifestation of a 5 year old vision which was almost lost in the noise of life. The vision was written and spoken as I ended my time at Fuller Youth Institute in 2015 when our class was prompted to write and share what we saw ourselves doing in 5 years.

I invite you to use the following pages to brainstorm, write, or draw in response to the following prompt: Where do you see yourself in 5 years?

_____

_____

_____

_____

_____

_____

_____

_____

_____

_____

_____

_____

_____

_____

_____

_____

_____

You have taken your first step, well done!

To contact me:

Writing the vision at different seasons in my life has been transformative, and encouraging others to do the same is something I am passionate about. I consider myself one of many midwives in our community working to birth visions to life. I am available for "Groanings from the Desert" readings, "Write the Vision" workshops, or other speaking or teaching opportunities and events that align with my experience and work. This includes but is not limited to community, women, and youth groups; within academic institutions, corporate, or non- profit organizations. I can be contacted through email almalizzette2020@gmail.com or my instagram @almalizzette_.

Para contactarme:

Escribir la visión en diferentes etapas de mi vida ha sido transformador, y animar a otros y otras a hacer lo mismo es algo que me apasiona. Me considero una de varias parteras en la comunidad trabajando para dar a luz las visiones de las mujeres y la juventud de la comunidad en especial. Para colaborar e invitaciones a sus eventos o espacios donde pueda leer de este libro, compartir mi historia, facilitar talleres que animen a su grupo o equipo a escribir su visión, y otras oportunidades que concuerden con mi experiencia y trabajo estoy disponible. Esto incluye y no está limitado a grupos de jóvenes, mujeres, y comunidades en instituciones académicas, corporaciones, y organizaciones sin fines de lucro. Comuníquese conmigo a almalizzette2020@gmail.com o por instagram @almalizzette_.

CPSIA information can be obtained
at www.ICGtesting.com
Printed in the USA
FSHW020959141220
76843FS